〈1

CHRISTIANITY
REDISCOVERED

IN PURSUIT OF GOD AND
THE PATH TO
ETERNAL LIFE

WHAT YOU NEED
TO KNOW TO GROW

LIVING THE CHRISTIAN LIFE
WITH JESUS CHRIST

MATHEW BACKHOLER

Christianity Rediscovered, in Pursuit of God and the Path to Eternal Life: What you Need to Know to Grow
Living the Christian Life with Jesus Christ, Book 1

All words of Scripture in italics are the author's own emphasis. As is the nature of the internet, web pages can disappear and ownership of domain names can change. Those stated within the book were valid at the time of first publication.

ISBN 978-1-907066-62-7 (paperback)
ISBN 978-1-907066-63-4 (eBook ePub)

British Library Cataloguing In Publication Data
A Record of this Publication is available from the British Library

Published in October 2018 by ByFaith Media

- Jesus Christ is Lord -

'For there is one God and one Mediator between God and men, the Man Christ Jesus, who gave Himself a ransom for all, to be testified in due time' (1 Timothy 2:5-6).

'And without controversy great is the mystery of godliness: God was manifested in the flesh, justified in the Spirit, seen by angels, preached among the Gentiles [non-Jews], believed on in the world, received up in glory' (1 Timothy 3:16).

God said, "I am the Lord your God, who divided the sea whose waves roared – the Lord of Hosts is His name" (Isaiah 51:15).

'...We trust in the living God, who is the Saviour of all men, especially of those who believe' (1 Timothy 4:10).

Jesus Christ said, "I am the Door. If anyone enters by Me, he will be saved, and will go in and out and find pasture. The thief [Devil] does not come except to steal, and to kill, and to destroy. I have come that they may have life, and that they may have it more abundantly. I am the good Shepherd. The good Shepherd gives His life for the sheep" (John 10:9-11).

Jesus Christ said, "Most assuredly, I say to you, whoever commits sin is a slave of sin. And a slave does not abide in the house forever, but a son abides forever. Therefore if the Son makes you free, you shall be free indeed" (John 8:34-36).

Contents

Appendices

Preface

"Give ear, O Heavens, and I will speak; and hear, O earth, the words of my mouth. Let my teaching drop as the rain, my speech distil as the dew, as raindrops on the tender herb, and as showers on the grass. For I proclaim the name of the Lord, ascribe greatness to our God. He is the Rock, His work is perfect; for all His ways are justice, a God of truth and without injustice; righteous and upright is He" (Deuteronomy 32:1-4).

"Then I saw a great white throne and Him [God] who sat on it, from whose face the earth and the Heaven fled away. And there was found no place for them. And I saw the dead, small and great, standing before God, and books were opened. And another book was opened, which is the Book of Life. And the dead were judged according to their works, by the things which were written in the books. The sea gave up the dead who were in it, and Death and Hades delivered up the dead who were in them. And they were judged, each one according to his works. Then Death and Hades were cast into the Lake of Fire. This is the second death. And anyone not found written in the Book of Life was cast into the Lake of Fire" (Revelation 20:11-15).

Since the beginning of time, mankind has asked, "What is life all about?" "Does my life matter?" And, "Is there an afterlife I can prepare for?" *Christianity Rediscovered* has the answers and much more. It reveals how to be in pursuit of God, gives focus, meaning, clarity, peace and direction to the path of eternal life, and shows how you can live the Christian life.

Christianity Rediscovered is rooted and grounded in the Word of God, the Bible and is written in an easy-to-read style with verses from the Bible printed in full with easy-to-understand explanations, practical advice and guidance. Intermingled throughout the book are short quotes from leaders of the Christian faith which help explain and reinforce Christian truth in a contemporary manner.

Each chapter starts with a question to set the scene and then proceeds to answer. At the end of each chapter, except the last one, are additional Bible References, if the reader chooses to delve deeper into each subject and topic covered. At the back of the book are Appendices, which gives the reader additional detail into different subjects within the book. There is also A Brief Overview of Each Book of the Bible, to give a broad spectrum of the Word of God and a Glossary of Terms as Christianity has much verbiage and theological phrases which to an outsider can be at first confusing.

Christianity Rediscovered begins by explaining mankind's need, our separation from God, the Creator of the universe and how we can be reconciled back to God through the finished work of Jesus Christ (God's son), who died on a cross, was buried, and rose from the grave so that we too can have eternal life in Him. Salvation is a free gift from God but we have to receive it by faith.

The book explains and reveals how you can become a Christian, what is expected of you and how best to live your life for Jesus Christ. The contents are practical in their explanations, lively in their illustrations and are not a list of do's and don'ts, but what you need to know.

Christianity Rediscovered explains what to do once you become a Christian and covers such vital subjects as: The Bible, Prayer, Attending a Place of Worship – Church, Communion – The Lord's Supper, Baptism in Water, Seven Biblical Words, Who I am In Christ Jesus, the Cost of Discipleship, Eternity and Living for Jesus Christ. These chapters reveal and demonstrate how you can live the Christian life and what you need to know to grow in the Christian faith, and to succeed in your walk with God.

The author became a Christian when he was ten years old and at the age of twenty-one he became serious with God and was baptised in water. A few years later he attended Bible College where he received theological training and went into fulltime Christian ministry. Twenty years have passed since enrolling at Bible College, the author has preached and taught at home and abroad and has written more than a dozen books since 2006.

The author is interdenominational in character, evangelical in outlook and believes that the Bible is the Word of God, and that Jesus Christ is the Son of God, the Saviour of the world. 'That there is no other name under Heaven given to men by which we must be saved.' The author exalts Jesus Christ and upholds Biblical truth whilst contending for the Christian faith.

'Be diligent to present yourself approved to God, a worker who does not need to be ashamed, rightly dividing the word of truth' (2 Timothy 2:15).

Chapter 1

In the Beginning – A look at Our Need

Jesus said, "Most assuredly, I say to you, he who hears My word and believes in Him [God] who sent Me has everlasting life, and shall not come into judgment, but has passed from death into life" (John 5:24).

'As it is written: "There is none righteous, no, not one" ' (Romans 3:10). 'Therefore by the deeds of the Law [Law of Moses, Old Testament rules and regulations] no flesh will be justified in His sight, for by the Law is the knowledge of sin' (Romans 3:20).

"Religion sounds boring, what can it mean to me?" For many people religion can be boring, dull and mundane, performing rituals and routines etc. to try and appease their god(s). However, Christianity is unique; it is about having a relationship with God (the Creator of the universe) and we can do that through His Son, Jesus Christ. We do not have to work or earn our way to God to seek His approval but God came and met mankind through Jesus Christ. You cannot earn or buy your salvation (the promise of eternal life in Heaven), as we could never do enough good deeds to pay the cost. Salvation is a free gift and it is found in Jesus Christ. God can forgive you of your sin, that is, all the wrong and bad things you have said, done and thought. Sin separates us from God, but Jesus Christ paid the price for mankind's sin by being crucified on a cross, taking the punishment we deserved so that we can be forgiven and set free.

- 'For the wages of sin is death, but the gift of God is eternal life in Christ Jesus our Lord' (Romans 6:23).
- 'Therefore, as through one man's offence [Adam] judgment came to all men, resulting in condemnation, even so through one Man's [Jesus Christ's] righteous act the free gift came to all men, resulting in justification of life' (Romans 5:18).

Christians believe in one God manifested in three: God the Father, God the Son (called Jesus, also known as Jesus Christ) and God the Holy Spirit (also known as the Holy Ghost or Spirit of God). They are known as the Trinity. God is the Creator of the Heavens and the earth and everything in it. (From the Bible, Genesis chapter 1-2, Genesis 1:2, 26, Matthew 28:19 and 1 John 5:7-8). The Bible is the world's best selling book and was also the first book to be printed. The Bible is split in two sections, the Old Testament and the New Testament, and consists of sixty-six books.

> Jesus said, "For God so loved the world that He gave His only begotten Son, that whoever believes in Him should not perish but have everlasting life. For God did not send His Son into the world to condemn the world, but that the world through Him might be saved" (John 3:16-17).

In the beginning Adam and Eve (the first humans) disobeyed God and this brought sin into the world. Sin is the wrong things that we do, say and think. Sin separates us from God. God wants to bring us back into a right relationship with Him and so sent His Son Jesus to earth. Jesus has existed since the beginning, as God is eternal. He could not just 'appear' as a man but had to be conceived, and grow up to identify with mankind. Mary who was a virgin, conceived by the Holy Spirit and Jesus was born on this earth as a baby. God did not have sex with Mary. Jesus had no sin and did not sin; He was from above (Heaven) and not from the line of Adam. Jesus grew into an adult and did many miracles, signs and wonders in the last three years of His life, as He went around telling people the Good News of eternal life and teaching people how to live. Jesus was wrongly accused, beaten, mocked, whipped then nailed to a wooden cross (crucified) where He died, and then was buried – however this was all part of God's plan, and after three days Jesus rose from the dead! Jesus died to take the punishment of mankind; when He hung on the cross, all the sins of the world were placed upon Him. You can find out more from the Bible. It is best if you start reading from the New Testament from the Book of Matthew.

- 'And the Word [Jesus] became flesh and dwelt among us, and we beheld His glory, the glory as of the only begotten of the Father, full of grace and truth' (John 1:14).
- John the Baptist saw Jesus coming toward him, and said, "Behold! The Lamb of God who takes away the sin of the world!" (John 1:29).

- 'For the Law was given through Moses, but grace and truth came through Jesus Christ' (John 1:17).
- Jesus said, "Most assuredly, I say to you, whoever commits sin is a slave of sin. And a slave does not abide in the house forever, but a son abides forever. Therefore if the Son makes you free, you shall be free indeed" (John 8:34-36).
- The apostle Paul wrote: 'Christ has redeemed us from the curse of the Law [the Law of Moses], having become a curse for us (for it is written, "Cursed is everyone who hangs on a tree," that the blessing of Abraham might come upon the Gentiles [non-Jews] in Christ Jesus, that we might receive the promise of the Spirit through faith' (Galatians 3:13-14).
- The apostle Paul wrote: 'Is the Law then against the promises of God? Certainly not! For if there had been a Law given which could have given life, truly righteousness would have been by the Law. But the Scripture has confined all under sin, that the promise by faith in Jesus Christ might be given to those who believe' (Galatians 3:21-22).

'For there is one God and one Mediator between God and men, the Man Christ Jesus, who gave Himself a ransom for all, to be testified in due time' (1 Timothy 2:5-6).

If you commit a crime, e.g. vandalism or theft and are caught, you can end up in a court of law and if found guilty, you could be fined or have a criminal record. You can plead your innocence but if a CCTV camera places you at the scene, or a witness, then it does not look good for you. You plead guilty and will have to accept the consequences; a fine, a suspended sentence or prison. But then the judge announces that although you are guilty he will pay the fine, or although you are deserving of imprisonment, you are free to go! That is mercy and grace, likewise, Jesus Christ paid the price for your freedom from eternal punishment so that you could go free, avoid Hell (a place of eternal darkness and torment, shut out from the presence of God) and go to Heaven when you die.
- Jesus said, "I am the Door. If anyone enters by Me, he will be saved, and will go in and out and find pasture. The thief [Devil] does not come except to steal, and to kill, and to destroy. I have come that they may have life, and that

they may have it more abundantly. I am the good Shepherd. The good Shepherd gives His life for the sheep" (John 10:9-11).

- 'Grace to you and peace from God the Father and our Lord Jesus Christ, who gave Himself for our sins, that He might deliver us from this present evil age, according to the will of our God and Father' (Galatians 1:3-4).
- Jesus said to His disciples, "Peace I leave with you, My peace I give to you; not as the world gives do I give to you. Let not your heart be troubled, neither let it be afraid" (John 14:27).

'Moreover, brethren, I declare to you the gospel which I preached to you, which also you received and in which you stand, by which also you are saved, if you hold fast that word which I preached to you – unless you believed in vain. For I delivered to you first of all that which I also received: that Christ died for our sins according to the Scriptures, and that He was buried, and that He rose again the third day according to the Scriptures' (1 Corinthians 15:1-4).

Quotes on Sin, the Devil and Jesus Christ
- The one business of the Devil is to damn. The one business of the Lord is to save – W. P. Nicholson, evangelist and revivalist.[1]
- Every time you say the word sin you can hear the hiss of the serpent – Gypsy Smith, evangelist and revivalist.
- All sin springs from one root cause – the refusal to have God ruling over us and telling us what to do – Selwyn Hughes, Bible teacher and founder of CWR.
- There are no little sins because there is no little God to sin against! – Selwyn Hughes.
- Don't blame your environment for your sin – look at Adam and Eve – Gypsy Smith.
- Jesus did for us what we could not do for ourselves – Lionel B. Fletcher, evangelist and revivalist.

Bible References: From the Bible, read the Gospels of Matthew, Mark, Luke and John, for information about Jesus Christ' life and mission – these are found in the New Testament. The punishment and victory of Jesus Christ as foretold in the Old Testament, Isaiah 53:1-12.

Chapter 2

What is a Christian?

'...So it was that for a whole year they [two apostles, Barnabas and Saul] assembled with the Church [at Antioch] and taught a great many people. And the disciples were first called Christians in Antioch' (Acts 11:25-26).

Jesus said, "And these will go away into everlasting punishment, but the righteous into eternal life" (Matthew 25:46).

"If I go to church does that make me a Christian?" No not at all. I go to the bathroom everyday and I have never turned into a toilet, sink or bathtub! When I walk into a garage it does not turn me into a car or a motorbike. Attending a church does not make you a Christian. Nobody has ever been born a Christian and God does not have grandchildren – only children. We can become children of God through our faith in Jesus Christ; by repenting and forsaking our sin, (the bad things we do, say, and think), and living for Jesus Christ.
- 'But as many as received Him [Jesus], to them He gave the right to become children of God, to those who believe in His name [Jesus]: who were born, not of blood, nor of the will of the flesh, nor of the will of man, but of God' (John 1:12-13).
- Jesus said, "Most assuredly, I say to you, unless one is born again, he cannot see the Kingdom of God" (John 3:3).

The word 'Christian' started as a nickname for the people who followed Jesus Christ and believed in His teaching. They belonged to that group of people; they were followers of Jesus Christ. Like Arabians, Grecians, Egyptians, Ethiopians, Corinthians, Ephesians etc. Christian means: followers of Jesus Christ or people belonging to Jesus. The name 'Christ' means Anointed One in the Greek language as that was the original language that most of the New Testament was written in.

New Christians are sometimes known as converts, because they converted to become followers of Jesus Christ. Christians are also known as: believers (for their faith in Jesus Christ), saints (for their holiness), brethren (for their love, because they are part of the family of God, brothers and sisters in Christ) and disciples (because of their knowledge and commitment to Christ). The first followers of Jesus Christ were known as disciples / apostles, and after a night of prayer, Jesus picked twelve who became known as the Twelve Disciples or the Twelve Apostles (Matthew 10:1-4 and Luke 6:12-16). See Appendix A. Other Christians in the New Testaments are known as apostles, often meaning 'sent ones,' like the apostle Paul, and they often performed signs and wonders in the name of Jesus Christ. Some Christians prefer to use the name 'disciple' rather than Christian, because Jesus said, "Go and make disciples..." (Matthew 28:19).

Jesus said, "I am the Bread of Life. He who comes to Me shall never hunger, and he who believes in Me shall never thirst" (John 6:35). "All that the Father gives Me will come to Me, and the one who comes to Me I will by no means cast out" (John 6:37). "Most assuredly, I say to you, he who believes in Me has everlasting life. I am the Bread of Life" (John 6:47-48).

Christians were also called followers of 'the way' (Acts 9:2 and Acts 24:14). People were first called 'Christians' in Antioch (Acts 11:26). It was like a church centre where the apostles were based whilst sharing the Good News further afield. Jerusalem was the centre of Christianity and the first mission sending base (Acts 11:19-22). To be a Christian you have to believe in Jesus, repent, forsake your sin (the bad things you say, do and think), receive Jesus by faith, and then apply His teaching to your life. Christians believe that the Bible is the inspired Word of God. If you call yourself a Christian, then you need to act like one or stop calling yourself a Christian.

- The apostle Peter declared, "Nor is there salvation in any other, for there is no other name under Heaven given to men by which we must be saved" (Acts 4:12). That name and Person is Jesus Christ.
- Jesus said, "I am the Way, and the Truth, and the Life. No one comes to the Father except through Me" (John 14:6).
- Jesus said, "Whoever drinks of the water that I shall give him will never thirst. But the water that I shall give him will

become in him a fountain of water springing up into everlasting life" (John 4:14).

Wearing a sport's shirt of one team and supporting another team does not make sense. You have to support the team whose shirt you are wearing. To wear Jesus Christ's 'shirt' as a Christian means you have to follow and obey Him. Jesus said, "If you love Me, keep My commandments" (John 14:15), and, "You are My friends if you do whatever I command you" (John 15:14). God is the Creator of the Heavens and the earth and all things in it; if you let Him guide your life then He will make a better go of it with you, than if you go it alone without Him. Jesus said, "For what will it profit a man if he gains the whole world and loses his own soul?" (Mark 8:36).

Jesus said, "Come to Me, all you who labour and are heavy laden, and I will give you rest. Take My yoke upon you and learn from Me, for I am gentle and lowly in heart, and you will find rest for your souls. For My yoke is easy and My burden is light" (Matthew 11:28-30).

J. Edwin Orr wrote: 'The English word "repentance" is very much misunderstood. The original Greek word, which is "metanoia," is a much stronger concept than is conveyed in its Latin or English translations. Repentance does not mean "feeling sorry." Rather it means to "changes one's thinking, change one's ways, change one's feelings."[1]

Repentance leads to salvation and without repentance there is no salvation! True repentance means a radical change of attitude towards God, and therefore towards sin. It is a genuine sorrow for sin, accompanied by a change of heart. It is an attitude of mind, as well as an act. Remorse...alone is not real repentance – Joe E. Church.[2]

For the truly repentant: He (or she) has a sincere grief for sin and a sincere hatred of sin. He used to live in sin, now he longs to be delivered from it. He used to love sin, now he loathes it. He used to revel in sin, now he runs from it. He used to delight in sin, now he detests it.

- 'For godly sorrow produces repentance leading to salvation...' (2 Corinthians 7:10).
- 'Repent therefore and be converted, that your sins may be blotted out, so that times of refreshing may come from the presence of the Lord' (Acts 3:19).

The Gospel in brief: The cross – sin, grace, faith, repent, forsake, believe, receive Jesus Christ; sealed by the Holy Spirit, justified (as if I had not sinned), sanctified (made holy), and later glorified (in Heaven). See Appendix B.

- 'And without controversy great is the mystery of godliness: God was manifested in the flesh, justified in the Spirit, seen by angels, preached among the Gentiles [non-Jews], believed on in the world, received up in glory' (1 Timothy 3:16).
- '...We trust in the living God, who is the Saviour of all men, especially of those who believe' (1 Timothy 4:10).

'But God demonstrates His own love toward us, in that while we were still sinners, Christ died for us. Much more then, having now been justified by His blood, we shall be saved from wrath through Him. For if when we were enemies we were reconciled to God through the death of His Son, much more, having been reconciled, we shall be saved by His life' (Romans 5:8-10).

Quotes on Repentance and Transformation
- Repentance is not promising to be better – it's not doing it again – Gypsy Smith.
- Light is not life and conviction is not repentance – Gypsy Smith.
- The Lord does not destroy personality, but transforms it – A. Lindsay Clegg, a businessman active in promoting Christianity.

Bible References. Old Testament: Ezekiel 18:20, Ezekiel 36:20, Jeremiah 29:13. New Testament: Mark 12:28-34, John 3:15-18, 36 and 2 Peter 2:4-9.

Jesus Christ the Saviour

- 'But God demonstrates His own love toward us, in that while we were still sinners, Christ died for us. Much more then, having now been justified by His blood, we shall be saved from wrath through Him' (Romans 5:8-9).
- Jesus said, "For God so loved the world that He gave His only begotten Son, that whoever believes in Him should not perish but have everlasting life" (John 3:16).
- Jesus said, "He who believes in the Son has everlasting life; and he who does not believe the Son shall not see life, but the wrath of God abides on him" (John 3:36).
- Jesus said, "For as the Father raises the dead and gives life to them, even so the Son gives life to whom He will" (John 5:21).

To be a Christian means you support Jesus Christ one hundred percent and you want to live your life for Him. You have been accepted into God's family and you are now a child of God. You can even call God, "Father" when you pray and talk to Him, 'But as many as received Him, to them He gave the right to become children of God, to those who believe in His name' (John 1:12). 'For you did not receive the spirit of bondage again to fear, but you received the Spirit of adoption by whom we cry out, "Abba, Father" ' (Romans 8:15). You should read a portion of your Bible everyday, pray daily (have a quiet time before God, private devotions), and try to live an upright life that glorifies God. Jesus said, "Most assuredly, I say to you, he who hears My word and believes in Him who sent Me has everlasting life, and shall not come into judgment, but has passed from death into life" (John 5:24).

'For though He [Jesus] was crucified in weakness, yet He lives by the power of God. For we also are weak in Him, but we shall live with Him by the power of God toward you. Examine yourselves as to whether you are in the faith. Test yourselves. Do you not know yourselves that Jesus Christ is in you? – unless indeed you are disqualified' (2 Corinthians 13:4-5).

Bible References. Old Testament: Psalm 143:10. New Testament: 1 Corinthians 6:9-10, Ephesians 2:8-9, and Revelation 3:20.

Chapter 5

Now I am a Christian

'It is good for me to draw near to God; I have put my trust in the Lord God, that I may declare all Your works' (Psalm 73:28).

'For we are His [God's] workmanship, created in Christ Jesus for good works, which God prepared beforehand that we should walk in them' (Ephesians 2:10).

"Now that I am a Christian, do I live my life waiting for Heaven?" No, living your life like that is like waiting for a bus; you never know when it will arrive. Heaven will come, but you have your whole life ahead of you, live it productively for God and for His glory. Jesus will come again, the Second Coming, and we must live as if He could come at anytime. We must be ready for His return (Matthew chapter 25). You can be happy because a mansion has been prepared for you in Heaven and you have a reservation!

Jesus said, "Let not your heart be troubled; you believe in God, believe also in Me. In My Father's house are many mansions; if it were not so, I would have told you. I go to prepare a place for you. And if I go and prepare a place for you, I will come again and receive you to Myself; that where I am, there you may be also" (John 14:1-3).

Christians are children of God and part of the family of believers (John 1:12). After you have given yourself to Jesus Christ, repented of your sins and put your trust in Him, you need to go and tell someone what you have done; you have decided to follow Jesus Christ. It could be a friend or relative, a work colleague or even a relative stranger, someone you met at the bus stop or a local shopkeeper.

- Jesus said, "Therefore whoever confesses Me before men, him I will also confess before My Father who is in Heaven" (Matthew 10:32).
- Jesus said, "Also I say to you, whoever confesses Me before men, him the Son of Man also will confess before the angels of God" (Luke 12:8).

set' (Proverbs 22:28). God has set boundaries to protect ourselves and others.

There are also cults which pretend to be Christian in nature, whilst their adherents may even call themselves Christian; however some of them have another book which to them is superior to the Bible. Stay away from cults. Cults do not adhere to orthodox Christianity, they often reject the deity of Jesus Christ, or the belief in Hell and try to earn their salvation by good works.

'As you therefore have received Christ Jesus the Lord, so walk in Him, rooted and built up in Him and established in the faith, as you have been taught, abounding in it with thanksgiving. Beware lest anyone cheat you through philosophy and empty deceit, according to the tradition of men, according to the basic principles of the world, and not according to Christ. For in Him dwells all the fullness of the Godhead bodily; and you are complete in Him, who is the head of all principality and power' (Colossians 2:6-10).

Churches often have denominational names like: Church of England, Presbyterian, Baptist, Methodist, United Reformed Church, Salvation Army, Pentecostal, Brethren, Episcopalian and Lutheran etc. Whenever you travel within your country or abroad you can still go to a church that you prefer, as the denominational churches are usually styled in the same format from one town or country to the next. Other churches are called by their ministry name or because of the street they are located on etc. There are many independent churches, without any affiliation to a larger organisation and lots of house churches, Christians who meet in homes.

Some church buildings can seem overwhelming, especially if you have never entered one before and you cannot see through the windows, but there is nothing to worry about. Most people turn up to church ten to twenty minutes before a service starts. There are often people on the door to greet visitors or to show people where to sit. Afterwards there may be tea and biscuits at the back of the church, in the church hall or another room. This is a good opportunity to meet other Christians in a social setting. Not all people who attend Church are Christian, some may be religious or curious, others may be searching for answers, it is a good place to keep warm in winter, or for some they could be looking for a potential place to get married.

Church styles and formats vary from place to place; sometimes a service is one hour long whereas in another church they will worship for one hour or more and then somebody will teach from the Bible for twenty minutes to one hour. The sermon is often presented by the pastor, vicar or church leader; however there may be a special visiting speaker or one of the church elders may preach. Each church has its own particular style but the object is to glorify God, to exalt Jesus Christ, to learn from the teaching of the Bible and to have fellowship with other Christians. Some churches are more traditional whereas others are pioneers. Some churches have a dress code, which is where the phrase "Sunday best" (clothes) came into being. Some churches wear formal wear (e.g. suits for men, or smart trouser and jacket), others are casual or smart casual. Generally, men do not wear a hat inside a church building, (however a Bishop can wear a mitre), but in some traditional churches they prefer it if a woman covers her head. This is more tradition, rather than Scriptural as a woman's covering is her hair (1 Corinthians 11:15). Wear what you feel comfortable wearing, though not too tight or too revealing. After you have been once, you can see if you were over or underdressed. You do not have to change to please other people, but you may feel more comfortable if you blend in.

- 'Walk prudently when you go to the house of God; and draw near to hear rather than to give the sacrifice of fools, for they do not know that they do evil' (Ecclesiastes 5:1).
- 'Only let your conduct be worthy of the gospel of Christ, so that whether I come and see you or am absent, I may hear of your affairs, that you stand fast in one spirit, with one mind striving together for the faith of the gospel' (Philippians 1:27).
- 'Husbands, love your wives, just as Christ also loved the church and gave Himself for her, that He might sanctify and cleanse her with the washing of water by the word, that He might present her to Himself a glorious church, not having spot or wrinkle or any such thing, but that she should be holy and without blemish. So husbands ought to love their own wives as their own bodies; he who loves his wife loves himself' (Ephesians 5:25-28).

The apostle Paul wrote: 'I now rejoice in my sufferings for you, and fill up in my flesh what is lacking in the afflictions of Christ, for the sake of His body, which is the Church, of which I became

Baptism Related Verses of Scripture

- 'Now I plead with you, brethren, by the name of our Lord Jesus Christ, that you all speak the same thing, and that there be no divisions among you, but that you be perfectly joined together in the same mind and in the same judgment. For it has been declared to me concerning you, my brethren, by those of Chloe's household, that there are contentions among you. Now I say this, that each of you says, "I am of Paul," or "I am of Apollos," or "I am of Cephas," or "I am of Christ." Is Christ divided? Was Paul crucified for you? Or were you baptised in the name of Paul? I thank God that I baptised none of you except Crispus and Gaius, lest anyone should say that I had baptised in my own name. Yes, I also baptised the household of Stephanas. Besides, I do not know whether I baptised any other. For Christ did not send me to baptise, but to preach the Gospel, not with wisdom of words, lest the cross of Christ should be made of no effect' (1 Corinthians 1:13-16).

- 'Moreover, brethren, I do not want you to be unaware that all our fathers were under the cloud, all passed through the sea, all were baptised into Moses in the cloud and in the sea, all ate the same spiritual food, and all drank the same spiritual drink. For they drank of that spiritual Rock that followed them, and that Rock was Christ' (1 Corinthians 10:1-4).

- 'Who is he who overcomes the world, but he who believes that Jesus is the Son of God? This is He who came by water and blood – Jesus Christ; not only by water, but by water and blood. And it is the Spirit who bears witness, because the Spirit is truth. For there are three that bear witness in Heaven: the Father, the Word [Jesus Christ], and the Holy Spirit; and these three are one. And there are three that bear witness on earth: the Spirit, the water, and the blood; and these three agree as one' (1 John 5:5-8).

Bible References. New Testament: Luke 3:3-18, Luke 7:29-30, Acts 9:17-22, Acts 16:25-33. The message of John the Baptist was a message of repentance, and to believe in the Coming One, the Messiah, Jesus Christ: Matthew 3:1-12, Acts 13:24-25, Acts 18:24-28 and Acts 19:1-7.

Chapter 11

Seven Biblical Words

'Do you not know that the unrighteous will not inherit the Kingdom of God? Do not be deceived. Neither fornicators, nor idolaters, nor adulterers, nor homosexuals, nor sodomites, nor thieves, nor covetous, nor drunkards, nor revilers, nor extortioners will inherit the Kingdom of God. And such were some of you. But you were washed, but you were sanctified, but you were justified in the name of the Lord Jesus and by the Spirit of our God' (1 Corinthians 6:9-11).

'But now the righteousness of God apart from the law is revealed, being witnessed by the Law and the Prophets, even the righteousness of God, through faith in Jesus Christ, to all and on all who believe. For there is no difference; for all have sinned and fall short of the glory of God, being justified freely by His grace through the redemption that is in Christ Jesus, whom God set forth as a propitiation by His blood, through faith, to demonstrate His righteousness, because in His forbearance God had passed over the sins that were previously committed, to demonstrate at the present time His righteousness, that He might be just and the justifier of the one who has faith in Jesus' (Romans 3:21-26).

In the Bible there are some biblical words which you may not understand. At the back of this book there is a Glossary of Terms, but in this chapter I will address the seven most common misunderstood theological terms for new Christians. Many of the verses reference one or more terms in each passage of Scripture because they are so intertwined.

'For Christ also suffered once for sins, the just for the unjust, that He might bring us to God, being put to death in the flesh but made alive by the Spirit' (1 Peter 3:18).

1. Atonement: At one with, peace has been made because of another's act. Jesus died on the cross, was buried and rose again, and made peace with God for our sins because of His sacrificial act on the cross of Calvary. We are redeemed because

of His sacrificial act of atonement. Jesus Christ made propitiation for our sins – He paid the price that God demanded so that God could be appeased. This is the plan of redemption that was decreed before the foundations of the earth were set in place!

- 'He [Jesus Christ] is despised and rejected by men, a Man of sorrows and acquainted with grief. And we hid, as it were, our faces from Him; He was despised, and we did not esteem Him. Surely He has borne our griefs and carried our sorrows; yet we esteemed Him stricken, smitten by God, and afflicted. But He was wounded for our transgressions, He was bruised for our iniquities; the chastisement for our peace was upon Him, and by His stripes we are healed. All we like sheep have gone astray; we have turned, every one, to his own way; and the Lord [God] has laid on Him [Jesus Christ] the iniquity of us all. He was oppressed and He was afflicted, yet He opened not His mouth; He was led as a lamb to the slaughter, and as a sheep before its shearers is silent, so He opened not His mouth' (Isaiah 53:3-7).

- 'Yet it pleased the Lord [God] to bruise Him [Jesus Christ]; He has put Him to grief. When You make His soul an offering for sin, He shall see His seed, He shall prolong His days, and the pleasure of the Lord shall prosper in His hand. He shall see the labour of His soul, and be satisfied. By His knowledge My righteous Servant shall justify many, for He shall bear their iniquities' (Isaiah 53:10-11).

- 'The priest shall make atonement for him, for his sin that he has committed in any of these matters; and it shall be forgiven him...' (Leviticus 5:13). In the Old Testament under the Old Covenant before Jesus Christ came to earth, animal sacrifices and obedience to more than six hundred laws and regulations were the only way to appease God. In the New Testament under the New Covenant, Jesus Christ was the sacrificial Lamb of God who made atonement to God and appeased Him through His suffering and shed blood on the cross.

- 'But Christ came as High Priest of the good things to come, with the greater and more perfect tabernacle not made with hands, that is, not of this creation. Not with the blood of goats and calves, but with His own blood He entered the Most Holy Place once for all, having obtained eternal redemption. For if the blood of bulls and goats and the ashes of a heifer, sprinkling the unclean, sanctifies for the purifying of the flesh, how much more shall the blood of Christ, who through the eternal Spirit offered Himself without spot to God, cleanse your conscience from dead works to serve the living God? And for this reason He is the Mediator of the New Covenant, by means of death, for the redemption of the transgressions under the first covenant, that those who are called may receive the promise of the eternal inheritance' (Hebrews 9:11-15).

- John the Baptist saw Jesus coming towards him, and said, "Behold! The Lamb of God who takes away the sin of the world!" (John 1:29).

- 'Therefore, if anyone is in Christ, he is a new creation; old things have passed away; behold, all things have become new. Now all things are of God, who has reconciled us to Himself through Jesus Christ, and has given us the ministry of reconciliation, that is, that God was in Christ reconciling the world to Himself, not imputing their trespasses to them, and has committed to us the word of reconciliation. Now then, we are ambassadors for Christ, as though God were pleading through us: we implore you on Christ's behalf, be reconciled to God. For He made Him who knew no sin to be sin for us, that we might become the righteousness of God in Him' (2 Corinthians 5:17-21).

2. Grace: Unmerited favour, something we don't deserve. It is God's gift to mankind which was outworked on the cross of Calvary, so that through faith in Jesus Christ we can be reconciled back to God. Someone came up with the acronym for grace: God's riches at Christ's expense.

- 'For all have sinned and fall short of the glory of God, being justified freely by His grace through the redemption that is in Christ Jesus, whom God set forth as a propitiation by His blood, through faith, to demonstrate His righteousness, because in His forbearance God had passed over the sins that were previously committed' (Romans 3:23-25).

- 'But the free gift is not like the offence. For if by the one man's offence many died, much more the grace of God and the gift by the grace of the one Man, Jesus Christ, abounded to many' (Romans 5:15).

- 'That in the ages to come He [God] might show the exceeding riches of His grace in His kindness toward us in Christ Jesus. For by grace you have been saved through faith, and that not of yourselves; it is the gift of God, not of works, lest anyone should boast' (Ephesians 2:7-9).

3. Washed in the blood: Spiritually we have been made clean from our sin, because Jesus Christ shed His blood for us and we can be reconciled back to God and have a relationship with Him. When we repent of our sin, God does not see our sin, our previous evil deeds, our dirty self, because Christ's blood has covered them. He sees us in white robes, clean and pure because He views us through Christ's act of redemption who shed His blood and paid the price for us.

- 'For it pleased the Father [God] that in Him [Jesus Christ] all the fullness should dwell, and by Him to reconcile all things to Himself, by Him, whether things on earth or things in Heaven, having made peace through the blood of His cross. And you, who once were alienated and enemies in your mind by wicked works, yet now He has reconciled' (Colossians 1:19-21).
- 'Much more then, having now been justified by His blood, we shall be saved from wrath through Him. For if when we were enemies we were reconciled to God through the death of His Son, much more, having been reconciled, we shall be saved by His life' (Romans 5:9-10).
- 'This is the message which we have heard from Him and declare to you, that God is light and in Him is no darkness at all. If we say that we have fellowship with Him, and walk in darkness, we lie and do not practice the truth. But if we walk in the light as He is in the light, we have fellowship with one another, and the blood of Jesus Christ His Son cleanses us from all sin. If we say that we have no sin, we deceive ourselves, and the truth is not in us. If we confess our sins, He is faithful and just to forgive us our sins and to cleanse us from all unrighteousness' (1 John 1:5-9).
- 'And from Jesus Christ, the faithful witness, the firstborn from the dead, and the ruler over the kings of the earth. To Him who loved us and washed us from our sins in His own blood' (Revelation 1:5).

James A. Stewart wrote: 'For a Christian redeemed by Calvary's blood to live a worldly life is treason and spiritual suicide.'

'Not by works of righteousness which we have done, but according to His mercy He saved us, through the washing of regeneration and renewing of the Holy Spirit' (Titus 3:5).

4. Sanctified: We have been made holy in God's eyes because of what Jesus Christ accomplished on the cross of Calvary.

- 'Sanctify them by Your truth. Your word is truth' (John 17:17).
- 'By that will [Jesus obeying God's will to be crucified for mankind's sins] we have been sanctified through the offering of the body of Jesus Christ once for all. And every priest stands ministering daily and offering repeatedly the same sacrifices, which can never take away sins. But this Man, after He had offered one sacrifice for sins forever, sat down at the right hand of God' (Hebrews 10:10-12).
- 'For the bodies of those animals, whose blood is brought into the sanctuary by the high priest for sin, are burned outside the camp. Therefore Jesus also, that He might sanctify the people with His own blood, suffered outside the gate [of Jerusalem's walls]' (Hebrews 13:11-12).

Oswald Chambers wrote: 'Sanctification costs to the extent of an intense narrowing of all our interests on earth and an immense broadening of all our interests in God.'

5. Justified: Just as if I had never sinned. It is as if we have never done wrong, just as if I never sinned because of Jesus Christ's finished work on the cross. Justified literally means: Just if I have not sinned.

- 'And the Scripture, foreseeing that God would justify the Gentiles [non-Jews] by faith, preached the gospel to Abraham beforehand, saying, "In you all the nations shall be blessed." So then those who are of faith are blessed with believing Abraham' (Galatians 3:8-9).
- 'Therefore the Law [Old Testament regulations] was our tutor to bring us to Christ, that we might be justified by faith' (Galatians 3:24).
- 'And the gift is not like that which came through the one who sinned. For the judgment which came from one offence resulted in condemnation, but the free gift which

salvation; in whom also, having believed, you were sealed with the Holy Spirit of promise, who is the guarantee of our inheritance until the redemption of the purchased possession, to the praise of His glory' (Ephesians 1:7-14).

In Christ I Am

The following are Scriptural statements and confessions about your status as a Christian:

1. I am *saved* by grace through faith. 'For by grace you have been saved through faith, and that not of yourselves; it is the gift of God' (Ephesians 2:8).

2. I am a *child of God* and an *heir* of God and *joint-heir* with Christ. 'The Spirit Himself bears witness with our spirit that we are children of God, and if children, then heirs – heirs of God and joint-heirs with Christ, if indeed we suffer with Him, that we may also be glorified together' (Romans 8:16-17). 'And because you are sons, God has sent forth the Spirit of His Son into your hearts, crying out, "Abba, Father!" Therefore you are no longer a slave but a son, and if a son, then an heir of God through Christ' (Galatians 4:6-7).

3. I am *redeemed* from the curse of the Law – the Old Testament regulations of animal sacrifices and observances. 'Christ has redeemed us from the curse of the Law, having become a curse for us (for it is written, "Cursed is everyone who hangs on a tree"), that the blessing of Abraham might come upon the Gentiles [non-Jews] in Christ Jesus, that we might receive the promise of the Spirit through faith' (Galatians 3:13-14).

4. I am an *heir of eternal life.* 'And this is the testimony: that God has given us eternal life, and this life is in His Son. He who has the Son has life; he who does not have the Son of God does not have life' (1 John 5:11-12).

5. I am *accepted* and *forgiven.* 'To the praise of the glory of His grace, by which He made us accepted in the Beloved. In Him we have redemption through His blood, the forgiveness of sins, according to the riches of His grace' (Ephesians 1:6-7).

6. I am *sanctified* and *justified* through Christ Jesus. 'And such were some of you. But you were washed, but you were sanctified, but you were justified in the name of the Lord Jesus and by the Spirit of our God' (1 Corinthians 6:11).

7. I am *justified* and at *peace* with God. 'Therefore, having been justified by faith, we have peace with God through our Lord Jesus Christ' (Romans 5:1).

8. I am at *peace* and can live in peace with God. Jesus said, "Peace I leave with you, My peace I give to you; not as the world gives do I give to you. Let not your heart be troubled, neither let it be afraid" (John 14:27).

9. I am *reconciled* to God. 'Much more then, having now been justified by His blood, we shall be saved from wrath through Him. For if when we were enemies we were reconciled to God through the death of His Son, much more, having been reconciled, we shall be saved by His life' (Romans 5:9-10).

10. I am *more than a conqueror.* 'Who shall separate us from the love of Christ? Shall tribulation, or distress, or persecution, or famine, or nakedness, or peril, or sword? As it is written: "For Your sake we are killed all day long; we are accounted as sheep for the slaughter." Yet in all these things we are more than conquerors through Him who loved us' (Romans 8:35-37).

11. I am *victorious.* "O death, where is your sting? O Hades [denoting a place of torment], where is your victory?" The sting of death is sin, and the strength of sin is the Law. But thanks be to God, who gives us the victory through our Lord Jesus Christ' (1 Corinthians 15:55-57).

12. I am *righteous* by faith in Jesus Christ. 'But now the righteousness of God apart from the law is revealed, being witnessed by the Law and the Prophets, even the righteousness of God, through faith in Jesus Christ, to all and on all who believe. For there is no difference' (Romans 3:21-22). 'For He [God] made Him [Jesus Christ] who knew no sin to be sin for us, that we might become the righteousness of God in Him' (2 Corinthians 5:21).

13. I am *healed by His wounds.* 'When evening had come, they [the people] brought to Him [Jesus Christ] many who were demon-possessed. And He cast out the spirits with a word, and healed all who were sick, that it might be fulfilled which was spoken by Isaiah the prophet, saying: "He Himself took our infirmities and bore our sicknesses" (Matthew 8:16-17). 'Who Himself [Jesus Christ] bore our sins in His own body on the tree, that we, having died to sins, might live for righteousness – by whose stripes you were healed' (1 Peter 2:24).

14. I have been delivered from the *wrath* to come. 'For they themselves declare concerning us what manner of entry we had to you, and how you turned to God from idols to serve the living and true God, and to wait for His Son from Heaven, whom He raised from the dead, even Jesus who delivers us from the wrath to come' (1 Thessalonians 1:9-10).

> 'Being confident of this very thing, that He who has begun a good work in you will complete it until the day of Jesus Christ' (Philippians 1:6).

If you were once a nobody then you are now a somebody in Christ. Jesus said, "If anyone desires to be first, he shall be last of all and servant of all" (Mark 9:35), and, "Many who are first will be last, and the last first" (Mark 10:31).

It is by His grace and mercy that we are accepted in the beloved. We must learn to live up to our royal position. Our position is by faith in Jesus Christ. Just because we are sanctified (made holy) does not give us a license to do what we want to do. We have our part to play by trying to live honourably before God. We choose to sin or not to sin. We should stand firm and not give in to temptation, resist the Devil and he will flee.

> 'Listen, my beloved brethren: has God not chosen the poor of this world to be rich in faith and heirs of the Kingdom which He promised to those who love Him?' (James 2:5).

Good Works
Good works and holiness are evidences of our salvation being out worked out in a practical way.

- 'For we are His workmanship, created in Christ Jesus for good works, which God prepared beforehand that we should walk in them' (Ephesians 2:10).
- 'Therefore, my beloved, as you have always obeyed, not as in my presence only, but now much more in my absence, work out your own salvation with fear and trembling; for it is God who works in you both to will and to do for His good pleasure. Do all things without complaining and disputing, that you may become blameless and harmless, children of God without fault in the midst of a crooked and perverse generation, among whom you shine as lights in the world, holding fast the word of life, so that I may rejoice in the day of Christ that I have not run in vain or laboured in vain' (Philippians 2:12-16).
- The apostle Paul wrote to Titus, a young Christian leader, who was establishing the Church (body of Christ) at Crete: 'In all things showing yourself to be a pattern of good works; in doctrine showing integrity, reverence,

incorruptibility, sound speech that cannot be condemned, that one who is an opponent may be ashamed, having nothing evil to say of you' (Titus 2:7-8).

- 'If you really fulfil the royal law according to the Scripture, "You shall love your neighbour as yourself," you do well' (James 2:8).
- Jesus Christ said, "Let your light so shine before men, that they may see your good works and glorify your Father in Heaven" (Matthew 5:16).
- The apostle Paul wrote to Timothy: 'Let no one despise your youth, but be an example to the believers in word, in conduct, in love, in spirit, in faith, in purity. Till I come, give attention to reading, to exhortation, to doctrine' (1 Timothy 4:12-13).

'Everyone who believes that Jesus is the Christ is born of God, and everyone who loves the father loves his child as well. This is how we know that we love the children of God: by loving God and carrying out His commands. In fact, this is love for God, to keep His commands. And His commands are not burdensome, for everyone born of God overcomes the world. This is the victory that has overcome the world, even our faith. Who is it that overcomes the world? Only the one who believes that Jesus is the Son of God' (1 John 5:1-5), NIV.

Soldiers of God

As Christians, disciples of the Lord we have been enlisted into God's army and are soldiers of the Lord. God is our supreme commander. We do not fight with weapons of the world, such as guns, knives or artillery, but we are in a spiritual battle against the powers of darkness who will try to assail on all fronts.

- 'Yet I considered it necessary to send to you Epaphroditus, my brother, fellow worker, and *fellow soldier,* but your messenger and the one who ministered to my need' (Philippians 2:25).
- 'You therefore must endure hardship as a *good soldier* of Jesus Christ. No one engaged in warfare entangles himself with the affairs of this life, that he may please him who enlisted him as a soldier. And also if anyone competes in athletics, he is not crowned unless he competes according to the rules' (2 Timothy 3-5).
- 'Finally, be strong in the Lord and in his mighty power. Put on the full armour of God, so that you can take your stand

against the Devil's schemes. For our struggle is not against flesh and blood, but against the rulers, against the authorities, against the powers of this dark world and against the spiritual forces of evil in the heavenly realms. Therefore put on the full armour of God, so that when the day of evil comes, you may be able to stand your ground, and after you have done everything, to stand. Stand firm then, with the belt of truth buckled around your waist, with the breastplate of righteousness in place, and with your feet fitted with the readiness that comes from the gospel of peace. In addition to all this, take up the shield of faith, with which you can extinguish all the flaming arrows of the evil one. Take the helmet of salvation and the sword of the Spirit, which is the word of God' (Ephesians 6:10-17), NIV.

- 'Then I heard a loud voice saying in Heaven, "Now salvation, and strength, and the Kingdom of our God, and the power of His Christ have come, for the accuser of our brethren [the Devil], who accused them before our God day and night, has been cast down. And they [Christians] overcame him by the blood of the Lamb and by the word of their testimony, and they did not love their lives to the death' (Revelation 12:10-11).

'Blessed be the God and Father of our Lord Jesus Christ, who according to His abundant mercy has begotten us again to a living hope through the resurrection of Jesus Christ from the dead, to an inheritance incorruptible and undefiled and that does not fade away, reserved in Heaven for you, who are kept by the power of God through faith for salvation ready to be revealed in the last time' (1 Peter 1:3-5).

Bible References: Old Testament: Psalm 68:19-20, Psalm 107:2-3, Isaiah 46:4 and Zechariah 3:1-6. New Testament: Matthew 5:14, 1 Corinthians 15:57, Colossians 1:13, Hebrews 11:7, James 4:7 and Revelation 12:11.

Chapter 13

The Cost of Discipleship

Jesus said, "If anyone desires to come after Me, let him deny himself, and take up his cross daily, and follow Me. For whoever desires to save his life will lose it, but whoever loses his life for My sake will save it. For what profit is it to a man if he gains the whole world, and is himself destroyed or lost? For whoever is ashamed of Me and My words, of him the Son of Man will be ashamed when He comes in His own glory, and in His Father's, and of the holy angels" (Luke 9:23-26).

Jesus said, "All authority has been given to Me in Heaven and on earth. Go therefore and make disciples of all the nations, baptising them in the name of the Father and of the Son and of the Holy Spirit, teaching them to observe all things that I have commanded you; and lo, I am with you always, even to the end of the age. Amen" (Matthew 28:18-20).

"What is the cost of being a Christian?" Salvation is a free gift from God, but God expects *all* of us, not just our hearts, but our dreams, emotions, desires, ambitions, our very wills. Some Christians are also persecuted for their faith in the Son of God whilst in some countries; believers may be beaten or killed for being a Christian, especially when they have converted from another religion and been baptised in water.

> The apostle Paul wrote to Timothy: 'But you have carefully followed my doctrine, manner of life, purpose, faith, longsuffering, love, perseverance, persecutions, afflictions, which happened to me at Antioch, at Iconium, at Lystra – what persecutions I endured. And out of them all the Lord delivered me. Yes, and all who desire to live godly in Christ Jesus will suffer persecution' (2 Timothy 3:10-12).

Once you have repented of your sins and accepted Jesus Christ as your Saviour, you then need to make Him your Lord. The Lord of your life, so that you are a vessel in His hands, a disciple of

Jesus Christ to do His will. It could be said that this is the small print, but with God He is open and honest and will not take advantage of you like a contract drawn-up by man. God knows best and can make more of your life than you can without Him.

Life is full of choices and we can accept Jesus Christ as our Saviour and Lord or reject Him and live for ourselves with its terrible consequences. It has been said that if Jesus is not Lord of *every* area of your life then He is not Lord at all. A disciple of Jesus Christ is a follower of Him and is somebody who truly wants to follow Jesus regardless of the cost. The cost can be high, but it is always worth it and the rewards are out of this world.

- Jesus said, "He who loves father or mother more than Me is not worthy of Me. And he who loves son or daughter more than Me is not worthy of Me. And he who does not take his cross and follow after Me is not worthy of Me. He who finds his life will lose it, and he who loses his life for My sake will find it" (Matthew 10:37-39).

- As they journeyed on the road, someone said to Jesus, "Lord, I will follow You wherever You go." And Jesus said to him, "Foxes have holes and birds of the air have nests, but the Son of Man has nowhere to lay His head." Then He said to another, "Follow Me." But he said, "Lord, let me first go and bury my father." Jesus said to him, "Let the dead bury their own dead, but you go and preach the Kingdom of God." And another also said, "Lord, I will follow You, but let me first go and bid them farewell who are at my house." But Jesus said to him, "No one, having put his hand to the plow, and looking back, is fit for the Kingdom of God" (Luke 9:57-62).

- The apostle Paul wrote: 'But what things were gain to me, these I have counted loss for Christ. Yet indeed I also count all things loss for the excellence of the knowledge of Christ Jesus my Lord, for whom I have suffered the loss of all things, and count them as rubbish, that I may gain Christ' (Philippians 3:7-8).

Jesus said, "It is the Spirit who gives life; the flesh profits nothing. The words that I speak to you are spirit, and they are life. But there are some of you who do not believe." For Jesus knew from the beginning who they were who did not believe, and who would betray Him. And He said, "Therefore I have said to you that no one can come to Me unless it has been granted to him by My

Father." From that time many of His disciples [not the twelve] went back and walked with Him no more. Then Jesus said to the twelve, "Do you also want to go away?" But Simon Peter answered Him, "Lord, to whom shall we go? You have the words of eternal life. Also we have come to believe and know that You are the Christ, the Son of the living God" (John 6:63-69).

Do your best to live for Jesus Christ, it is a life-long process but you have to start somewhere. You will make mistakes, ask God to forgive you and move on (Proverbs 24:16). Even some Bible characters made grave errors but still accomplished much. These mistakes and negative experiences have not been air-brushed from the Bible, but are written for our learning. When you are unsure what to do, ask yourself, "What would Jesus do?"

To live like Jesus we need to follow His example as found in the four Gospels, (the first four books of the New Testament: Matthew, Mark, Luke and John), as these chronicle Jesus' birth, His life on earth, his teaching, healings, miracles, death, burial, resurrection and commission (go and tell other people). Obey the Scriptures and you will get results; violate them and you will get consequences. God has a plan and purpose for your life and He knows best. We have a Helper, the Comforter, the Spirit of Truth, called the Holy Spirit. He can help us understand the Bible, to glorify Jesus Christ and convict us when we do wrong.

The Holy Spirit
- Jesus said, "But the Helper, the Holy Spirit, whom the Father will send in My name, He will teach you all things, and bring to your remembrance all things that I said to you" (John 14:26).
- Jesus said, "Nevertheless I tell you the truth. It is to your advantage that I go away; for if I do not go away, the Helper will not come to you; but if I depart, I will send Him to you. And when He has come, He will convict the world of sin, and of righteousness, and of judgment: of sin, because they do not believe in Me; of righteousness, because I go to My Father and you see Me no more; of judgment, because the ruler of this world is judged. I still have many things to say to you, but you cannot bear them now. However, when He, the Spirit of Truth, has come, He will guide you into all truth; for He will not speak on His own authority, but whatever He hears He will speak; and He will tell you things to come. He will glorify Me, for He

Healing evangelist, George Jeffreys wrote: 'Be out and out for Christ, let there be no half-measures in all your undertakings for Him. Give much of your time to prayer and the reading of God's Word. Be determined to claim every promise in the Scripture that is made to believers. Give implicit obedience to every one of its commands. Embrace every opportunity of presenting the truth of salvation to others. Enter every open door of service that you might minister in His name. Seek at all times to follow Christ as your example in life. You have been born again to live for Him. You have enlisted under His banner for active service, you have been saved to serve. Remember that true happiness in the Christian life can only be enjoyed to the measure that you pursue the happiness of others for His sake. May the marks of the first early Church converts be conspicuous in your life. They received and obeyed His word with gladness, they continued steadfastly in the Apostles' doctrines, they enjoyed the fellowship of saints, they remembered their absent Lord in the breaking of bread and they loved the prayer meetings.'[4]

'Therefore, if anyone is in Christ, he is a new creation; old things have passed away; behold, all things have become new' (2 Corinthians 5:17).

Live the Life

I'd rather see a sermon than hear one any day,
I'd rather one would walk with me than merely tell the way;
The eye's a better pupil, more willing than the ear,
Fine counsel is confusing, but example's always clear;
   The best of all the preachers are the men who live their creeds,
   For to see good put in action is what everybody needs;
I soon can learn to do it if you'll let me see it done,
I can watch your hands in action, but your tongue too fast may run;
   The lectures you deliver may be very wise and true,
   But I'd rather get my lesson by observing what you do;
I may not understand the high advice that you may give,
But there's no misunderstanding how you act and how you live.
– Anonymous.

Barnabas, 'When he came and had seen the grace of God, he was glad, and encouraged them all that with purpose of heart they should continue with the Lord' (Acts 11:23).

The apostle Paul wrote to young Timothy: 'Be diligent to present yourself approved to God, a worker who does not need to be ashamed, rightly dividing the Word of truth' (2 Timothy 2:15).

Holiness

- 'Give unto the Lord the glory due to His name; worship the Lord in the beauty of holiness' (Psalm 29:2).
- 'Examine me, O Lord, and prove me; try my mind and my heart' (Psalm 26:2).
- 'Search me, O God, and know my heart; try me, and know my anxieties; and see if there is any wicked way in me, and lead me in the way everlasting' (Psalm 139:23-24).
- 'Create in me a clean heart, O God, and renew a steadfast spirit within me' (Psalm 51:10).
- 'For they indeed for a few days chastened [disciplined] us as seemed best to them, but He for our profit, that we may be partakers of His holiness' (Hebrews 12:10).
- 'Pursue peace with all people, and holiness, without which no one will see the Lord' (Hebrews 12:14).

The way from the higher state to the very highest is very much watered by tears. I do not believe any man will ever come to be an advanced Christian except by sorrowing much for sin – C. H. Spurgeon, known as the Prince of Preachers.

Holiness – Body Parts

- Eyes: 'I have made a covenant with my eyes; why then should I look upon a young woman?' (Job 31:1). 'My eyes are ever towards the Lord, for He shall pluck my feet out of the net' (Psalm 25:15). 'Better is the sight of the eyes than the wandering of desire...' (Ecclesiastes 6:9).
- Mouth: '...I have purposed that my mouth shall not transgress' (Psalm 17:3).
- Lips and tongue: 'My lips will not speak wickedness, nor my tongue utter deceit' (Job 27:4).
- Ears: 'Your ears shall hear a word behind you, saying, "This is the way, walk in it," whenever you turn to the right hand or whenever you turn to the left' (Isaiah 30:21).
- Hearing and Speaking: 'So then, my beloved brethren, let every man be swift to hear, slow to speak, slow to wrath;

for the wrath of man does not produce the righteousness of God' (James 1:19-20).

- Hands and heart: 'Who may ascend into the hill of the Lord? Or who may stand in His holy place? He who has clean hands and a pure heart...' (Psalm 24:3-4).
- Body and spirit: 'For you were bought at a price; therefore glorify God in your body and in your spirit which are God's' (1 Corinthians 6:20).
- Words and heart: 'Let the words of my mouth and the meditation of my heart be acceptable in Your sight, O Lord, my strength and my Redeemer' (Psalm 19:14).

Holiness and Wisdom in Quotes

- What you dislike in another take care to correct in yourself – Thomas Sprat.
- If you don't get the better of yourself, someone else will – Anonymous.
- No matter how far you have gone on a wrong road, turn back – Turkish proverb.
- There are sinners saved by grace and sinners who serve Satan. One has faith in the Saviour, whilst the other serves self.
- The purpose of the Church is to gather, through her testimony of truth and love, a people who, saved by grace, and separated by the Holy Ghost [Holy Spirit] from the world are serving the Lord and waiting for His coming (1 Thessalonians 1) – James A. Stewart.
- You cannot live in sin and die in grace.

A minister asked a Christian who was seeking church membership, how things were in his new life. "Fine" said the believer, "but I still can't come to terms with the things I have to give up." The pastor replied, "Stop thinking about the things you have to give up and think of what Christ gave up for you."

We are saved to serve, not for self. We are called to do the will of God, not our own will. The flesh profits nothing, but the Spirit quickens. We are not to continue in the flesh but to walk in the Spirit, not to have fellowship with darkness, but with those in the light.

Whilst most people have natural limitations, most people never attempt to work to their full potential and would be amazed at what is possible if only they stepped out in faith. Never allow fear of the unknown to paralyse you; worse than fear is coming to the end of your life and saying, "If only?" In the walk of faith, the impossible becomes the possible and the mountain becomes a molehill. Live your life for God, and when your time is up you will not be disappointed at the eternal rewards. There is much in life to be learnt and the best education you can get is in the college of life.

Trust God and love Him with all your heart, mind, soul and strength; exalt and honour Jesus Christ through your life, daily, as well as through your words and thoughts, and be obedient to the Holy Spirit.

'Blessed be the God and Father of our Lord Jesus Christ, who according to His abundant mercy has begotten us again to a living hope through the resurrection of Jesus Christ from the dead, to an inheritance incorruptible and undefiled and that does not fade away, reserved in Heaven for you, who are kept by the power of God through faith for salvation ready to be revealed in the last time. In this you greatly rejoice, though now for a little while, if need be, you have been grieved by various trials, that the genuineness of your faith, being much more precious than gold that perishes, though it is tested by fire, may be found to praise, honour, and glory at the revelation of Jesus Christ, whom having not seen you love. Though now you do not see Him, yet believing, you rejoice with joy inexpressible and full of glory, receiving the end of your faith – the salvation of your souls' (1 Peter 1:3-9).

Thank you for reading this book, please write a short (or long) review on your favourite review site, and give a shout-out on social media – thank you.

www.ByFaith.co.uk

www.RevivalNow.co.uk

www.MissionsNow.co.uk

again, he cannot see the Kingdom of God" (John 3:3). "Do not marvel that I said to you, 'You must be born again' " (John 3:7). Jesus said, "And I will pray the Father, and He will give you another Helper, that He may abide with you forever – the Spirit of Truth [Holy Spirit], whom the world cannot receive, because it neither sees Him nor knows Him; but you know Him, for He dwells with you and will be in you" (John 14:16-17). 'Who also has sealed us and given us the Spirit in our hearts as a guarantee' (2 Corinthians 1:22). 'In Him [Jesus] you also trusted, after you heard the word of truth, the Gospel of your salvation; in whom also, having believed, you were sealed with the Holy Spirit of promise' (Ephesians 1:13). 'And do not grieve the Holy Spirit of God, by whom you were sealed for the day of redemption' (Ephesians 4:30). '...Our Lord Jesus Christ...that He would grant you...that Christ may dwell in your hearts through faith...' (Ephesians 3:14, 16-17). 'The solid foundation of God stands, having this seal: "The Lord knows those who are His," and, "Let everyone who names the name of Christ depart from iniquity" ' (2 Timothy 2:19).

- We must respond to the call of the Spirit and the Bride (the Church) and come. 'And the Spirit and the Bride say, "Come!" And let him who hears say, "Come!" And let him who thirsts come. Whoever desires, let him take the water of life freely' (Revelation 22:17).

- We must respond with sincere repentance. John the Baptist declared, "Repent, for the Kingdom of Heaven is at hand!" (Matthew 3:2). Jesus said, "Repent, for the Kingdom of Heaven is at hand" (Matthew 4:17).

- Paul wrote: 'We are saved by grace, through faith, it is a gift from God. For by grace you have been saved through faith, and that not of yourselves; it is the gift of God, not of works, lest anyone should boast' (Ephesians 2:8-9).

- The Holy Spirit bears witness that we are children of God. 'But as many as received Him, [Jesus] to them He gave the right to become children of God, to those who believe in His name: who were born, not of blood, nor of the will of the flesh, nor of the will of man, but of God' (John 1:12-13). Jesus said, "But when the Helper [Holy Spirit] comes, whom I shall send to you from the Father, the Spirit of Truth who proceeds from the Father, He will testify of Me" (John 15:26).

The Holy Spirit in the Plan of Redemption

- God the Father gave His Son. Jesus said, "For God so loved the world that He gave His only begotten Son, that whoever believes in Him should not perish but have everlasting life. For God did not send His Son into the world to condemn the world, but that the world through Him might be saved" (John 3:16-17).

- Jesus the Son volunteered to come. Jesus said, "Therefore My Father loves Me, because I lay down My life that I may take it again. No one takes it from Me, but I lay it down of Myself. I have power to lay it down, and I have power to take it again. This command I have received from My Father" (John 10:17-18).

- The Holy Spirit prepared the way. 'Therefore, when He [Jesus] came into the world, He said, "Sacrifice and offering You [God] did not desire, but a body, You have prepared for Me" ' (Hebrews 10:5).

- Jesus was born of the Holy Spirit. The angel Gabriel said to the Virgin Mary, "The Holy Spirit will come upon you, and the power of the Highest will overshadow you; therefore, also, that Holy One who is to be born [Jesus] will be called the Son of God" (Luke 1:35).

- Genuine Christians are born of the Spirit. 'But as many as received Him, to them He gave the right to become children of God, to those who believe in His name: who were born, not of blood, nor of the will of the flesh, nor of the will of man, but of God' (John 1:12-13). Jesus said, "Most assuredly, I say to you, unless one is born of water and the Spirit, he cannot enter the Kingdom of God. That which is born of the flesh is flesh, and that which is born of the Spirit is spirit. Do not marvel that I said to you, 'You must be born again' " (John 3:5-7).

- We come under conviction of sin by the Holy Spirit. Jesus said, "And when He [Holy Spirit] has come, He will convict the world of sin, and of righteousness, and of judgment" (John 16:8).

- Christians will be raised to life by the Holy Spirit. 'The eyes of your understanding being enlightened; that you may know what is the hope of His calling, what are the riches of the glory of His inheritance in the saints, and what is the exceeding greatness of His power toward us who believe, according to the working of His mighty power which He worked in Christ when He raised Him

Historical and Adventure

Britain, A Christian Country, A Nation Defined by Christianity and the Bible & the Social Changes that Challenge this Biblical Heritage by Paul Backholer. For more than 1,000 years Britain was defined by Christianity, with monarch's dedicating the country to God and national days of prayer. Discover this continuing legacy, how faith defined its nationhood and the challenges from the 1960s till today.

How Christianity Made the Modern World, The Legacy of Christian Liberty: How the Bible Inspired Freedom and Shaped Western Civilization by Paul Backholer. Christianity is the greatest reforming force that the world has ever known, yet its legacy is seldom comprehended. The author brings this legacy alive by revealing how Christianity revolutionized human rights, transformed democracy, shaped our values and beliefs, helped create the path that led to Western liberty and laid the foundations of the modern world.

Celtic Christianity & the First Christian Kings in Britain: From St. Patrick and St. Columba, to King Ethelbert and King Alfred by Paul Backholer. Celtic Christians ignited a Celtic Golden Age of faith and light which spread into Europe. Discover this striking history and what we can learn from the heroes of Celtic Christianity.

Lost Treasures of the Bible: Exploration and Pictorial Travel Adventure of Biblical Archaeology by Paul Backholer. Join a photographic quest in search of the lost treasures of the Bible. Unveil ancient mysteries as you discover the evidence for Israel's Exodus from Egypt, and travel into lost civilisations in search of the Ark of the Covenant. Explore lost worlds with over 160 colour pictures in the paperback edition and find how evidence outside of the Bible gives a deeper insight into the mysteries of ancient Israel.

The Exodus Evidence In Pictures – The Bible's Exodus: The Hunt for Ancient Israel in Egypt, the Red Sea, the Exodus Route and Mount Sinai by Paul Backholer. Two brothers and explorers, Paul and Mathew Backholer search for archaeological data to validate the biblical account of Joseph, Moses and the Hebrew Exodus from ancient Egypt. With more than 100 full colour photos and graphics in the paperback edition.

The Ark of the Covenant – Investigating the Ten Leading Claims by Paul Backholer. The mystery of the Bible's lost Ark of the Covenant has led to many myths, theories and claims. Join two explorers as they investigate the ten major theories concerning the location of antiquities greatest relic. Combining an on-site travel journal with

80+ colour photographs (in the paperback edition), through Egypt, Ethiopia and beyond.

Short-Term Missions (Christian Travel with a Purpose)
Short-Term Missions, A Christian Guide to STMs: For Leaders, Pastors, Churches, Students, STM Teams and Mission Organizations – Survive and Thrive by Mathew Backholer. A full and concise guide to short-term missions (STMs). What you need to know about planning a STM, or joining a STM team, and considering the options as part of the Great Commission, from the Good News to good works. This book is full of anecdotes and advice with informative timelines, and a biblical framework for STMs to help you engage in cross-cultural missions; with viable solutions to common mission issues to make your STM more effective to the glory of God.

How to Plan, Prepare and Successfully Complete Your Short-Term Mission: For Churches, Independent STM Teams and Mission Organizations by Mathew Backholer. This book will guide you through all you need to know about your short-term mission (STM): the why and how to, the cost, raising money, who can go, reconnaissance, what to take and what to do (Good News and good works), team work, safety and security, and includes: the Scriptural basis for STMs, mission statistics, quotes and more than 140 real-life STM testimonies.

Revivals and Spiritual Awakenings
Revival Fires and Awakenings, Thirty-Six Visitations of the Holy Spirit: A Call to Holiness, Prayer and Intercession for the Nations by Mathew Backholer. With 36 fascinating accounts of revivals in nineteen countries from six continents, plus biblical teaching on revival, prayer and intercession. Also available as a hardback.

Global Revival, Worldwide Outpourings, Forty-Three Visitations of the Holy Spirit: The Great Commission, Revivals in Asia, Africa, Europe, North & South America, Australia and Oceania by Mathew Backholer. This book documents forty-three revivals from more than thirty countries on six continents. The author explores the Divine-human partnership of revival, explains how revivals are birthed, and reveals the fascinating links between pioneering missionaries and the revivals that they saw as they worked towards the Great Commission.

Understanding Revival and Addressing the Issues it Provokes So that we can Intelligently Cooperate with the Holy Spirit during times of *Revivals and Awakenings* by Mathew Backholer. Many who have prayed for revival have rejected it when it came because they misunderstood the workings of the Holy Spirit and only wanted God to bless the Church on their terms and not His. Let us intelligently cooperate with the Holy Spirit during times of revivals, Heaven-sent spiritual awakenings and not reject His workings or be misled by the enemy.

Revival Fire, 150 Years of Revivals, Spiritual Awakenings and Moves of the Holy Spirit: Days of Heaven on Earth by Mathew Backholer. This book documents in detail, twelve revivals from ten countries on five continents. Through the use of detailed research, eye-witness accounts and interviews, *Revival Fire* presents some of the most potent revivals that the world has seen in the past one hundred and fifty years. Learn from the past, be challenged for the present and be inspired for the future!

Revival Answers, True and False Revivals, Genuine or Counterfeit Do not be Deceived: Discerning Between the Holy Spirit and the Demonic by Mathew Backholer. What is genuine Heaven-sent revival and how can we tell the true from the spurious? Drawing from Scripture with examples across Church history, this book will sharpen your senses and take you on a journey of discovery. See the Holy Spirit at work in true Heaven-sent revivals!

Reformation to Revival, 500 Years of God's Glory: Sixty Revivals, Awakenings and Heaven-Sent Visitations of the Holy Spirit by Mathew Backholer. For the past five hundred years God has been pouring out His Spirit, to reform and to revive His Church. *Reformation to Revival* traces the Divine thread of God's power from Martin Luther of 1517, through to the Charismatic Movement and into the twenty-first century, featuring sixty great revivals from twenty nations on five continents, plus teaching on Heaven-sent revivals.

Christian Teaching and Inspirational
Jesus Today, Daily Devotional: 100 Days with Jesus Christ by Paul Backholer. Two minutes a day to encourage and inspire; 100 days of daily Christian Bible inspiration to draw you closer to God. Have you ever wished you could have sat at Jesus' feet and heard Him speak? Now you can. *Jesus Today* is a concise daily devotional defined by the teaching of Jesus and how His life can change yours. See the world from God's perspective and live abundantly in Christ!

Holy Spirit Power: Knowing the Voice, Guidance and Person of the Holy Spirit by Paul Backholer. Power for Christian living; drawing from the powerful influences of many Christian leaders, including: Rees Howells, Evan Roberts, D. L. Moody, Duncan Campbell and other channels of God's Divine fire.

Samuel Rees Howells: A Life of Intercession: The Legacy of Prayer and Spiritual Warfare of an Intercessor by Richard Maton is an in-depth look at the intercessions of Samuel Rees Howells alongside the faith principles that he learnt from his father, Rees Howells, and under the leading and guidance of the Holy Spirit. With 39 black and white photos in the paperback and hardback editions.

Tares and Weeds in Your Church: Trouble & Deception in God's House, the End Time Overcomers by R. B. Watchman. Is there a battle taking place in your house, church or ministry, leading to division? Tares and weeds are counterfeit Christians used to sabotage Kingdom work; learn how to recognise them and neutralise them in the power of the Holy Spirit.

The Baptism of Fire, Personal Revival, Renewal and the Anointing for Supernatural Living by Paul Backholer. Jesus will baptise you with the Holy Spirit and fire; that was the promise of John the Baptist. But what is the baptism of fire and how can you experience it? In this book, the author unveils the life and ministry of the Holy Spirit, shows how He can transform your life and what supernatural living in Christ means. Filled with biblical references, testimonies from heroes of the faith and the experiences of everyday Christians, you will learn that the baptism of fire is real and how you can receive it!

Supernatural and Spiritual
Glimpses of Glory, Revelations in the Realms of God Beyond the Veil in the Heavenly Abode: The New Jerusalem and the Eternal Kingdom of God by Paul Backholer. Find a world beyond earth which is real, vivid and eternal. Many people have claimed to have visited Heaven and yet these accounts often conflict with what the Word of God says. In this narrative receive biblical glimpses and revelations into life in paradise, which is filled with references to Scripture to confirm its veracity. A gripping read!

Prophecy Now, Prophetic Words and Divine Revelations for You, the Church and the Nations by Michael Backholer. An enlightening end time prophetic journal of visions, prophecies and words from the Holy Spirit to God's people, the Church and the nations.

Heaven, A Journey to Paradise and the Heavenly City by Paul Backholer. Join one person's exploration of paradise, guided by an angel and a glorified man, to witness the thrilling promise of eternity, and to provide answers to many questions about Heaven. Anchored in the Word of God, the Bible, discover what Heaven will be like!

Biography and Autobiography
The Holy Spirit in a Man: Spiritual Warfare, Intercession, Faith, Healings and Miracles by R. B. Watchman. One man's compelling journey of faith and intercession – a gripping true-life story. Raised in a dysfunctional family and called for a Divine purpose, he ran from God, yet the world could not break nor tame him. Years later, he met with Christ in power through a dynamic encounter with the Holy Spirit and was changed forever. Sent out by God, he left employment to claim the ground for Christ, witnessing signs and wonders, spiritual warfare and deliverance. In a remarkable modern day story of miracles and faith, see how God can take a depressed, defeated individual, teach him faith and use him for His glory.

Samuel, Son and Successor of Rees Howells: Director of the Bible College of Wales – A Biography by Richard Maton. The author invites us on a lifelong journey with Samuel, to unveil his ministry at the College, life of prayer and the support he received from numerous staff, students and visitors, as the history of BCW unfolds alongside the Vision to reach Every Creature with the Gospel. With 113 black and white photos in the paperback and hardback editions!

Budget Travel – Holiday/Vacations
Budget Travel, a Guide to Travelling on a Shoestring, Explore the World, a Discount Overseas Adventure Trip: Gap Year, Backpacking, Volunteer-Vacation and Overlander by Mathew Backholer. *Budget Travel* is a practical and concise guide to travelling the world and exploring new destinations with fascinating opportunities and experiences. Full of anecdotes, traveller's advice, informative timelines and testimonies, with suggestions, guidance, ideas and need-to-know information to help you survive and thrive on your budget travels and have the adventure of a lifetime! Whether you go solo, join with friends, participate in humanitarian work, join an overland bus trip or take your own vehicle, this book is for you.

www.ByFaithBooks.co.uk

ByFaith Media DVDs

Revivals and Spiritual Awakenings

Great Christian Revivals on 1 DVD is an inspirational and uplifting account of some of the greatest revivals in Church history. Filmed on location across Britain and drawing upon archive information, the stories of the Welsh Revival (1904-1905), the Hebridean Revival (1949-1952) and the Evangelical Revival (1739-1791) are brought to life in this moving 72-minute documentary. Using computer animation, historic photos and depictions, the events of the past are weaved into the present, to bring these Heaven-sent revivals to life.

Christian Travel (Backpacking Style Short-Term Mission)

ByFaith – World Mission on 1 DVD is a Christian reality TV show that reveals the real experience of a backpacking style short-term mission in Asia, Europe and North Africa. Two brothers, Paul and Mathew Backholer shoot through fourteen nations, in an 85-minute real-life documentary. Filmed over three years, *ByFaith – World Mission* is the very best of ByFaith TV season one.

Historical and Adventure

Israel in Egypt – The Exodus Mystery on 1 DVD. A four year quest searching for Joseph, Moses and the Hebrew slaves in Egypt. Join Paul and Mathew Backholer as they hunt through ancient relics and explore the mystery of the biblical Exodus, hunt for the Red Sea and climb Mount Sinai. Discover the first reference to Israel outside of the Bible, uncover depictions of people with multicoloured coats, encounter the Egyptian records of slaves making bricks and find lost cities. 110 minutes. *Israel in Egypt* is the very best of ByFaith TV season two, *ByFaith – In Search of the Exodus*.

ByFaith – Quest for the Ark of the Covenant on 1 DVD. Join two adventurers on their quest for the Ark, beginning at Mount Sinai where it was made, to Pharaoh Tutankhamun's tomb, where Egyptian treasures evoke the majesty of the Ark. The quest proceeds onto the trail of Pharaoh Shishak, who raided Jerusalem. The mission continues up the River Nile to find a lost temple, with clues to a mysterious civilization. Crossing through the Sahara Desert, the investigators enter the underground rock churches of Ethiopia, find a forgotten civilization and examine the enigma of the final resting place of the Ark itself. 100+ minutes.

www.ByFaithDVDs.co.uk